This Pet Journal Belongs To:
Daisy Tessa Russell

MY PET *Profile*

NAME: Daisy

BREED: Cockapoo

BIRTHDAY: 23.05.20

GENDER: Girl (female)

ID CHIP #:

ALLERGIES:

COAT COLOR: chocolate/creme/white

EYE COLOR:

SPECIAL MARKINGS: chocolate ring around tail.

MEDICAL CONDITIONS:

WEIGHT:

FAVORITE TOYS: All of them

SPAY/NEUTERED:	YES:	NO:
NOTES:		

Vet Information

NAME/BUSINESS:

PHONE:

EMAIL:

ADDRESS:

Groomer Information

NAME/BUSINESS:

PHONE:

EMAIL:

ADDRESS:

PET Vaccination Chart

YEAR:

PET NAME:		DOB:	GENDER:

VACCINATION HISTORY

DATE:	VACCINATION:	AGE:	NOTES:

VETERINARY CARE *Tracker*

DATE:	DESCRIPTION:	LOCATION:	AMOUNT:

PET HEALTH
Immunization Records

DATE:	AGE:	TYPE:	GIVEN BY:	NEXT DUE:

PET HEALTH
Medication Records

DATE:	AGE:	MEDICATION:	GIVEN BY:	NEXT DUE:

PET MEDICATION *Tracker*

DATE & TIME:	MEDICATION:	FREQUENCY:	DOSAGE:

PET WELLNESS *Journal*

YEAR:

PET NAME:	DOB:	GENDER:

WELLNESS HISTORY

DATE:	DESCRIPTION:	TREATMENT:	NOTES:

PET SITTER *Notes*
- RESPONSIBILITIES -

	M	T	W	T	F	S	S

MONTH: _____ **YEAR:** _____

PET NAME: _____

EXPENSE TRACKER

DATE	FOOD	VET	MEDICATION	GROOMING	COST
					$
					$
					$
					$
					$
					$
					$
					$
					$
					$
					$
					$
					$
					$
					$
					$
					$

MONTH: **YEAR:**

PET NAME:

EXPENSE TRACKER

DATE	FOOD	VET	MEDICATION	GROOMING	COST
					$
					$
					$
					$
					$
					$
					$
					$
					$
					$
					$
					$
					$
					$
					$
					$
					$

MONTHLY PET *Overview*

JANUARY

FEBRUARY

MARCH

APRIL

MAY

JUNE

MONTHLY PET *Overview*

JULY	AUGUST	SEPTEMBER

OCTOBER	NOVEMBER	DECEMBER

WEEKLY PET *Journal*

WEEK OF: _____

MONDAY	TUESDAY	WEDNESDAY

THURSDAY	FRIDAY	SATURDAY

SUNDAY	WEEKLY NOTES

MY PET Journal

WEEKLY PET *Journal*

WEEK OF: _____

MONDAY	TUESDAY	WEDNESDAY

THURSDAY	FRIDAY	SATURDAY

SUNDAY	WEEKLY NOTES

MY PET Journal

WEEKLY PET *Journal*

WEEK OF: _____

MONDAY	TUESDAY	WEDNESDAY

THURSDAY	FRIDAY	SATURDAY

SUNDAY	WEEKLY NOTES

MY PET Journal

WEEKLY PET *Journal*

WEEK OF: _____

MONDAY	TUESDAY	WEDNESDAY

THURSDAY	FRIDAY	SATURDAY

SUNDAY	WEEKLY NOTES

MY PET Journal

WEEKLY PET *Journal*

WEEK OF: _____

MONDAY	TUESDAY	WEDNESDAY

THURSDAY	FRIDAY	SATURDAY

SUNDAY	WEEKLY NOTES

MY PET Journal

WEEKLY PET *Journal*

WEEK OF: _____

MONDAY	TUESDAY	WEDNESDAY

THURSDAY	FRIDAY	SATURDAY

SUNDAY	WEEKLY NOTES

MY PET Journal

WEEKLY PET *Journal*

WEEK OF: _____

MONDAY	TUESDAY	WEDNESDAY

THURSDAY	FRIDAY	SATURDAY

SUNDAY	WEEKLY NOTES

MY PET Journal

WEEKLY PET *Journal*

WEEK OF: _____

MONDAY	TUESDAY	WEDNESDAY

THURSDAY	FRIDAY	SATURDAY

SUNDAY	WEEKLY NOTES

MY PET Journal

WEEKLY PET *Journal*

WEEK OF: _____

MONDAY	TUESDAY	WEDNESDAY

THURSDAY	FRIDAY	SATURDAY

SUNDAY	WEEKLY NOTES

MY PET Journal

WEEKLY PET *Journal*

WEEK OF: _____

MONDAY	TUESDAY	WEDNESDAY

THURSDAY	FRIDAY	SATURDAY

SUNDAY	WEEKLY NOTES

MY PET Journal

WEEKLY PET *Journal*

WEEK OF: _____

MONDAY	TUESDAY	WEDNESDAY

THURSDAY	FRIDAY	SATURDAY

SUNDAY	WEEKLY NOTES

MY PET Journal

WEEKLY PET *Journal*

WEEK OF: _____

MONDAY	TUESDAY	WEDNESDAY

THURSDAY	FRIDAY	SATURDAY

SUNDAY	WEEKLY NOTES

MY PET Journal

WEEKLY PET *Journal*

WEEK OF: _____

MONDAY	TUESDAY	WEDNESDAY

THURSDAY	FRIDAY	SATURDAY

SUNDAY	WEEKLY NOTES

MY PET Journal

WEEKLY PET *Journal*

WEEK OF: _____

MONDAY	TUESDAY	WEDNESDAY

THURSDAY	FRIDAY	SATURDAY

SUNDAY	WEEKLY NOTES

MY PET Journal

WEEKLY PET *Journal*

WEEK OF: _____

MONDAY	TUESDAY	WEDNESDAY

THURSDAY	FRIDAY	SATURDAY

SUNDAY	WEEKLY NOTES

MY PET Journal

WEEKLY PET *Journal*

WEEK OF: _____

MONDAY	TUESDAY	WEDNESDAY

THURSDAY	FRIDAY	SATURDAY

SUNDAY	WEEKLY NOTES

MY PET Journal

WEEKLY PET *Journal*

WEEK OF: _____

MONDAY	TUESDAY	WEDNESDAY

THURSDAY	FRIDAY	SATURDAY

SUNDAY	WEEKLY NOTES

MY PET Journal

WEEKLY PET *Journal*

WEEK OF: _____

MONDAY	TUESDAY	WEDNESDAY

THURSDAY	FRIDAY	SATURDAY

SUNDAY	WEEKLY NOTES

MY PET Journal

WEEKLY PET *Journal*

WEEK OF: _____

MONDAY	TUESDAY	WEDNESDAY

THURSDAY	FRIDAY	SATURDAY

SUNDAY	WEEKLY NOTES

MY PET Journal

WEEKLY PET *Journal*

WEEK OF: _____

MONDAY	TUESDAY	WEDNESDAY

THURSDAY	FRIDAY	SATURDAY

SUNDAY	WEEKLY NOTES

MY PET Journal

WEEKLY PET *Journal*

WEEK OF: _____

MONDAY	TUESDAY	WEDNESDAY

THURSDAY	FRIDAY	SATURDAY

SUNDAY	WEEKLY NOTES

MY PET Journal

WEEKLY PET *Journal*

WEEK OF: _____

MONDAY	TUESDAY	WEDNESDAY

THURSDAY	FRIDAY	SATURDAY

SUNDAY	WEEKLY NOTES

MY PET Journal

WEEKLY PET *Journal*

WEEK OF: _____

MONDAY	TUESDAY	WEDNESDAY

THURSDAY	FRIDAY	SATURDAY

SUNDAY	WEEKLY NOTES

MY PET Journal

WEEKLY PET *Journal*

WEEK OF: _____

MONDAY	TUESDAY	WEDNESDAY

THURSDAY	FRIDAY	SATURDAY

SUNDAY	WEEKLY NOTES

MY PET Journal

WEEKLY PET *Journal*

WEEK OF: _____

MONDAY	TUESDAY	WEDNESDAY

THURSDAY	FRIDAY	SATURDAY

SUNDAY	WEEKLY NOTES

MY PET Journal

WEEKLY PET *Journal*

WEEK OF: _____

MONDAY	TUESDAY	WEDNESDAY

THURSDAY	FRIDAY	SATURDAY

SUNDAY	WEEKLY NOTES

MY PET Journal

WEEKLY PET *Journal*

WEEK OF: _____

MONDAY	TUESDAY	WEDNESDAY

THURSDAY	FRIDAY	SATURDAY

SUNDAY	WEEKLY NOTES

MY PET Journal

WEEKLY PET *Journal*

WEEK OF: _____

MONDAY	TUESDAY	WEDNESDAY

THURSDAY	FRIDAY	SATURDAY

SUNDAY	WEEKLY NOTES

MY PET Journal

WEEKLY PET *Journal*

WEEK OF: _____

MONDAY	TUESDAY	WEDNESDAY

THURSDAY	FRIDAY	SATURDAY

SUNDAY	WEEKLY NOTES

MY PET Journal

WEEKLY PET *Journal*

WEEK OF: _____

MONDAY	TUESDAY	WEDNESDAY

THURSDAY	FRIDAY	SATURDAY

SUNDAY	WEEKLY NOTES

MY PET Journal

WEEKLY PET *Journal*

WEEK OF: _____

MONDAY	TUESDAY	WEDNESDAY

THURSDAY	FRIDAY	SATURDAY

SUNDAY	WEEKLY NOTES

MY PET Journal

WEEKLY PET *Journal*

WEEK OF: _____

MONDAY	TUESDAY	WEDNESDAY

THURSDAY	FRIDAY	SATURDAY

SUNDAY	WEEKLY NOTES

MY PET Journal

WEEKLY PET *Journal*

WEEK OF: _____

MONDAY	TUESDAY	WEDNESDAY

THURSDAY	FRIDAY	SATURDAY

SUNDAY	WEEKLY NOTES

MY PET Journal

WEEKLY PET *Journal*

WEEK OF: _____

MONDAY	TUESDAY	WEDNESDAY

THURSDAY	FRIDAY	SATURDAY

SUNDAY	WEEKLY NOTES

MY PET Journal

WEEKLY PET *Journal*

WEEK OF: _____

MONDAY	TUESDAY	WEDNESDAY

THURSDAY	FRIDAY	SATURDAY

SUNDAY	WEEKLY NOTES

MY PET Journal

WEEKLY PET *Journal*

WEEK OF: _____

MONDAY	TUESDAY	WEDNESDAY

THURSDAY	FRIDAY	SATURDAY

SUNDAY	WEEKLY NOTES

MY PET Journal

WEEKLY PET *Journal*

WEEK OF: _____

MONDAY	TUESDAY	WEDNESDAY

THURSDAY	FRIDAY	SATURDAY

SUNDAY	WEEKLY NOTES

MY PET Journal

WEEKLY PET *Journal*

WEEK OF: _____

MONDAY	TUESDAY	WEDNESDAY

THURSDAY	FRIDAY	SATURDAY

SUNDAY	WEEKLY NOTES

MY PET Journal

WEEKLY PET *Journal*

WEEK OF: _____

MONDAY	TUESDAY	WEDNESDAY

THURSDAY	FRIDAY	SATURDAY

SUNDAY	WEEKLY NOTES

MY PET Journal

WEEKLY PET *Journal*

WEEK OF: _____

MONDAY	TUESDAY	WEDNESDAY

THURSDAY	FRIDAY	SATURDAY

SUNDAY	WEEKLY NOTES

MY PET Journal

WEEKLY PET *Journal*

WEEK OF: _____

MONDAY	TUESDAY	WEDNESDAY

THURSDAY	FRIDAY	SATURDAY

SUNDAY	WEEKLY NOTES

MY PET Journal

WEEKLY PET *Journal*

WEEK OF: _____

MONDAY	TUESDAY	WEDNESDAY

THURSDAY	FRIDAY	SATURDAY

SUNDAY	WEEKLY NOTES

MY PET Journal

WEEKLY PET *Journal*

WEEK OF: _____

MONDAY	TUESDAY	WEDNESDAY

THURSDAY	FRIDAY	SATURDAY

SUNDAY	WEEKLY NOTES

MY PET Journal

WEEKLY PET *Journal*

WEEK OF: _____

MONDAY	TUESDAY	WEDNESDAY

THURSDAY	FRIDAY	SATURDAY

SUNDAY	WEEKLY NOTES

MY PET Journal

WEEKLY PET *Journal*

WEEK OF: _____

MONDAY	TUESDAY	WEDNESDAY

THURSDAY	FRIDAY	SATURDAY

SUNDAY	WEEKLY NOTES

MY PET Journal

WEEKLY PET Journal

WEEK OF: _____

MONDAY	TUESDAY	WEDNESDAY

THURSDAY	FRIDAY	SATURDAY

SUNDAY	WEEKLY NOTES

MY PET Journal

WEEKLY PET *Journal*

WEEK OF: _____

MONDAY	TUESDAY	WEDNESDAY

THURSDAY	FRIDAY	SATURDAY

SUNDAY	WEEKLY NOTES

MY PET Journal

WEEKLY PET *Journal*

WEEK OF: _____

MONDAY	TUESDAY	WEDNESDAY

THURSDAY	FRIDAY	SATURDAY

SUNDAY	WEEKLY NOTES

MY PET Journal

WEEKLY PET *Journal*

WEEK OF: _____

MONDAY	TUESDAY	WEDNESDAY

THURSDAY	FRIDAY	SATURDAY

SUNDAY	WEEKLY NOTES

MY PET Journal

WEEKLY PET *Journal*

WEEK OF: _____

MONDAY	TUESDAY	WEDNESDAY

THURSDAY	FRIDAY	SATURDAY

SUNDAY	WEEKLY NOTES

MY PET Journal

WEEKLY PET *Journal*

WEEK OF: _____

MONDAY	TUESDAY	WEDNESDAY

THURSDAY	FRIDAY	SATURDAY

SUNDAY	WEEKLY NOTES

MY PET Journal

WEEKLY PET *Journal*

WEEK OF: _____

MONDAY	TUESDAY	WEDNESDAY

THURSDAY	FRIDAY	SATURDAY

SUNDAY	WEEKLY NOTES

MY PET Journal

MY PET Journal

MY PET Journal

Printed in Great Britain
by Amazon